Paperback ISBN: 978-0-578-25080-9

LILY OF THE NILE

A fragrance of Love and Virtue

Matthew Edeh

ACKNOWLEDGEMENTS

To my friends and family and everyone
who supported the growth of Pen Mysteries. I will forever be indebted
to the almighty God for grace and inspiration who is my very source of
existence, my mother, ma'am Teresa James, Emerie and ma'am Abigail
and not forgetting my humble friends Shiekuma and Sarah Coles.
I am grateful for your unending support and encouragement.

TABLE OF CONTENTS

The Grace of a Man

I am a man
I am brave down to the grave
I am the pillar that bears the house
I am stronger than an ox
Mouth less in speech
My mouth I open to preach and teach.

I am a man
Out of me was the tree that bears fruits
I am a son from the dust
I was the mirror of truth
Broken by deception of pride in my root
I am who I want to be.

I am a man
A husband and a father
A controller and a ruler
I am the head upholding heads
A river and a shade
I sacrifice to satisfy.

I am a man
I am the sun to my family
I lead the way like the moon at night
A custodian and a guardian
My heart shifts with joy when respected
I am the pills of love.

I am a man
Admired and desired
In pleasure our feet treasure
Yet our pressure is beyond measure
Our bed endowed under the shadow of adventure
Survival evolved from the taste of my sweat
My impact is undisputed.

The Grace of a Woman

I am a woman
I am bold like an aquiline
So strong like the lion
I am the spin that rotates the earth
The pride that rocks glamour.

I am a woman
A keeper and a partner
We build a home but I maintain the house
I am powerful
I am a ruler.

I am a woman
I am special reborn
Crafted from the crib of the rib
I am the frail that trap men
I am stronger than my weakness.

I am a woman
Grace and gifted
Raised to be praised
Loved and cherished
Blessed and appreciated.

I am a woman
Full of affections and emotions
I am a mother
Caring and loving
I am who I am
I am a woman.

Mona Lisa

I have made my heart a gallery of you
For I do believe that pictures don't lie
Stuck with my ink and paper
Painting your face in styles and patterns
Your countenance
The light in my lantern
I will continue to paint
In complex of colours and lattice
Till the world is made a picture of you.

Solace

I will keep looking for you
As the sun cast her stare on me
I will ramshackle the cloud
Unclad the stars.

Like a hunter searching for his hunt
Oh earth, where have you taken him to?
I will keep checking for you
Whispering my message to the wind
Hoping her passing drops it on your mind
My legs will never sleep until you are found
My peace I dash to the streets
As my heart runs through cities.

I will keep awakening for you
The moon wouldn't sleep in her tent
Ceasing the day from the breath of content
My wailing would be sang with a bang
Untamed and unstable as the sea
My bones would never be weary
My faith stream would never be dry.

If Wishes Come True

I wish I could swim this ocean
Just to be with you for a moment
I wish I could fly across the galaxy
Just to hold you.

I wish I could pass through this darkness
Just to feel the rays of your beauty over my face
I wish I could jump every hurdle
Just to hear the sound of your heart beat.

I wish I could break this wall
Just to embrace you for a minute
I wish I could run through this jungle
Just to spend the day by your side.

I wish I could climb over this mountain
Just to kiss your lips throughout the night
I wish I can sail through this storm
Just to feel your skin on mine.

I wish I can swift with the wind
Just to dwell in your bosom
I wish I can fight through this hurricane
Just to be pinned down with you
Oh, if wishes were horses
How I wish, wishes come true.

With You

Don't care if the sun shine in her full strength
Being with you is enough
Even on a stormy night
My fears are hidden
Being in your arms keeps me calm.

Striding in the rain
Dancing to the claps of shivering
Being with you is like bathing in the glory of the moon
Though the world go mad
Fazed and gloomy
I find comfort as I come forth
Into the tent of my heartbeat.

Petal of roses at Dawn
Hug and kisses at dusk
Every day with you is like a magical experience,
that leaves me breathless
My desire is you in me
For all of me
Want all of you.

Lily at the Nile

On the island of stir and admiration
I met a lily at the Nile
There were signs of love and smile from a mile
And I was lost in the flow of sensation.

At the cast of her glimpse
My day was made beautiful
Filled with the glory of the sun.

There were echoes of happiness hovering beyond resistance
Their steps were felt on the desolated streets in my heart
My world was made empty at your sight.

Striking the pool of sweet melodies
Your voice whispers into my depth
So soft and sweet
Like chocolate, cream, and butter.

Walk with me my sunshine
Let's jab our fears
So our heart will glee
Like riding on horses
Let's rollercoaster buggy on the Love highway
Stay closer as we rock the way.

Sexy Ceci

Days of wrappers are over
Obstinacy in decency
Farewell, oh my fairest long skirt.

She is a star of fashion
Rocking bikini
Soaking deeper in leggings fiestas.

Mansion in a posh
Preening and primping
Her lips, she dips in blood.

Manicure and pedicure she incurred
Majestic steps she counts
She is embraced by a new world.

She races in haste
After her new looks she caste
New hook and nook ups.

She perched on every trend
She is quiet and quaint
In her world sexiness is reborn.

Grandma's Kitchen

Where smoke never stops rising
Where fire never stops burning
Where pots are always black.

Grandma's kitchen
A place where plates sing
Where the stomach don't think
Jingle the teeth let hunger fling.

Grandma's kitchen
From the porch and every spot are filled with teaching
A place where the spoon always visits the pot.

Grandma's kitchen
My comfort zone
My joy cone
Where my strength is upheld.

Grandma's kitchen
My heart desire from afar
Where my legs run to in par
Nothing like grandma's kitchen.

Grandma's kitchen
Free and sumptuous
The key that strengthens the mouth
In her domain things don't far apart.

Dream Chasers

We live by ambition
Succeed by determination
Exist by persisting.

We look to climb the highest peak
Ready to swim the deepest ocean and conven,
the longest distances to meet up demands.

We are desperate beings
Consuming any chance like wildfire
Setting our eyes on nothing else but the goals,
and targets to actualize.

Our soul is as thirsty as a vampire
Longing each day and night
To suck from the breast of achievement.

We are strong and auspicious
Having no room for giving in to any restrictions,
and impediments
For our ambition must come into action.

Chance

I had the bruise
Because I had no feet.

Down the street
I met a man who had no feet.

So often it happens
Living lives in chains while we have the keys.

We are all in the gutter of the lost
Casting hope as a call to touch the sky.

Journey raided by acceptance of who you are
Bare of self-contempt in the tent.

Brace and open up the passage of your heart to chance
Soaring through the cloud of enthusiasm.

Losses are not counted
But chances are recounted.

Anywhere is Paradise
It's up to you to load the dice.

Trapped

I thought I would never fall for love again
I thought my heart was sealed from her sting
Yet just a stare from her caught me again
Suddenly I am drowning in her again.

Her spell enslaved me to her gain
Gradually I was drawn back to her main
My weakness has found strength to regain
Her thoughts now filled my mind like rain.

Love is powerful
Her drop makes our lives meaningful,
and colorful like a peacock
Her presence makes lives joyful and beautiful
When abused she becomes hurtful
We live under her every day.

Spell of Love

Love is like a circular flow
Blowing to and fro like the wind
She is felt and when touched melts like ice.

You can't live without her feels
Her wings heal
Her strike deals
Her breath steals
Holding hearts captive.

She is the beauty of songs played with the string of the heart
She has driven millions of minds crazy
Free, but hard to find her true nature.

She is gold
The load carried by feelings
She is stronger than an ox
Opaque beyond comprehension.

She gives life
She is regardless
Capturing both the old and you
She is a panacea
A drop of her can end the longest enmity.

She quenches engulfed aversion
As she showcases the nature of divinity
She portrays an identity
She is blind, because she sees no fault.

Love is purer than gold
She is stronger than cold
She doesn't get old.

Love is godly
She is patient
She awaits the right time to satisfy self-pleasure
She never derives happiness in sinfulness but truthfulness
She doesn't withhold but give all in her fullness.

She doesn't behave rudely, enviously, selfishly, and with jealousy
Love is everlasting
Love never fails.

A New Dawn

Goodbye to the guns and knives
Let our shame be gone and let our peace be won.

Goodbye to the household of greed
We are setting off with a new deed.

Goodbye to the race of racism
For the forest doesn't carry one tree.

Goodbye to the treat of threat
We would think peace for all to find rest.

It is due we empty our cups
Our hearts would stand tall like the mountains.

We are ready to uphold a new dawn
In fullness and newness.

We are moving to our new home
A place where Love would reign.

Agony of Leah

I am a voice crying in the desert
I am a song sang in the dark
I am a lost coin without a seeker
I am Leah.

I am that thirsty river
My tears flowed as my soul shivered
I am the evidence of hope undelivered
I am Leah.

I am the rejected dream from a distance
Suffocated by the world of my mother
My tunes would ever be heard by the night like an owl
I am Leah.

I am the fount of pains
I was exposed to be seen by the eyes of sin
I was savouring pangs as a next of kin
I am Leah.

Oh mother nature I heard your heart calling
Mop the streams from your eyes
Your streets are filled with blood already
I will return to you when my eyes are closcd steady
I am Leah.

I am that stolen seed
Taken far beyond where hands can intercede
My mother was deprived of the joy of motherhood
I am Leah.

Did the world pray for me
Did she mourn with me
Was I really meant for her
Let her set my story as a tombstone
Because I am Leah.

A Stand with Love

Come oh earth and drink from her pour
Fill out your bellies till the last hour
Open up to harbour the seed of love
Only she can offer comfort in joy.

Your eyes have seen chaos caused by the hands
Your ear can testify of the cruel ire of the mouth
It is time to free yourself from the cleft that rid your sanity
Will you remain enslaved to hate forever?

It is time to start a new chapter
Detach every notes of the old songs
For her verses are full of lines of commotion and frustration
Rip off the old cargo of malice.

Rinse yourself of her dust and walk to the love gate
In her hides melodies of pleasures
Her fruits are gain with no pains
She offers beauty for ashes.

Nothing is something that doesn't stay forever
Embrace now the arms of change that she offers
It is time to rebuild every broken walls
Let's stand up for a new era.

Searching for Love

Does true love really exist?
Love that will feed on patience
Love that wouldn't give up on another pretense
Love that would drain under the rain of care.

Love that reads the heartbeat
Love that defends
Love that doesn't wine with fend.

Love that doesn't bloom in greed
Love that ego is rid
Love that is kind and leading.

If true love really exists
I will wait and insist
I will be open and persist
For I wish to find her someday.

Found Love

I have finally found my fish that was lost in the sea
I have found my missing treasure
My heart rejoices with great measures
We are the true definition of perfection.

My scratch story has ended in glory
In all instances my lip will always say sorry
My promises will never decay
The flames of our love would never die in a hurry.

Black Diamond

Her skin is her Pride
Is it her fault that she's black?
It is a mystery behind the door
That will only be known when the hen laughs with her teeth.
Her black is not a spot gotten like that of a leopard
All the water in river Nile cannot wash her.

Black is the proud Lion of Africa
Many eyes keep looking at us
We are not the cause so don't curse
You can't remove her for she's the rock of gibraltar
Either you bend or you break
Oh great black!

The silent thunder
For many years you've struggle
Weep no more for success will soon smile on you
Let not her appearance come to judgement
Her primitive interior is pregnant with deep secrets
Can the gun survive without the hole?

Give her liberty or give her death
Speech is silver but silence is gold
She's always bold until she get old
Love her and be her truth.

Falling Stars

We started on a right page
Our love grew stronger like age.

We flow in talks to bind our hearts in cage
Oh love!!!
Have you suddenly gone off stage?

In a blink distance was created
My heart is getting cold
But she is still melted by thoughts trooping in her hut.

I am shot by hurt
And I am short of words
For I was shot by love.

Gloomy Reflection

Was my heart a grocery?
Why did you steal from it?
You broke in like a pandemic
Robbing me of every tool that speaks joy and comfort.

Why give up on me now?
Why has the love that once tasted like honey
Stir up sweeter than bile?
I yearn for you every night
Your touch that struck like a magic wand
Healing every spot my heart ever felt pain.

I remembered my last tears
Trooping down like the fountain fall
Hoping you stay with me after all.

We were bound in the shackles of love
You held my hands
Looked deep into my eyes
Unsealed your lips and spoke to me of unspoken love
Was our love not meant to be?

Together we were yet not bonded
My heart beat of an unquenched affection
Singing the unabated love she has for you to the moon
Dreaming about the night that never dawned
For a hand that is far beyond my reach,
As long as I breath
This feeling will etch for eternity.

Shattered

Am tired of chasing after you
No more will I fool around.

Let love spit on my face no more
Am surrounded by the pleasure of heartbreak.

I will tell my story to the stars
Singing my songs in stupor to the air.

Bask my worries to the sun
With silence I will be a friend.

I will stand and watch
Not to touch at such
For a wall has been built in between us
Our hearts have gone cold.

Sweet memories trashed in fold
Flux is perplexed untold.

Now playing cards on the table
No more cage in affections.

When the blood of love dries off my vein
Then will I sleep in my stream of tears.

Virtuous Woman

A real woman is a mother to all
Her arms are like a cave of safety
Answerable to all who call
There is competence and impartiality in her wall.

With what will she be replaced?
She worth more than a house filled with rubies
Even the wealth of Solomon would get sold
But her replacement can't be told.

With her hands she keep the world in place
She gives her family portion at the gate
She has no room for strife and hate.

Her lamp doesn't sleep at night
Oh! What a woman of good tides
Her legs are always hitting the road
To gather little but enough to sustain her family.

Her knees are strengthened like the strength of a stone
Restless until happiness is ensured
Her mouth supplies breath of wisdom
Like a night watcher
She examines the ways of her household.

Her teeth have never grinded the bread of idleness
Millions of her children call her blessed
Though many daughters did well
But she excels them all
When many seasons have seen the sun
She will be praised and raised by her own at the gate.

Woman-fully

Woman of valor
Only she knows the magic between the pot and fire
At the wiggling of her fingers every stomach smiles.

House of gold
She is a shelter for the young and old
Her smiles sparkled with care and affection that are untold.

Mother of the world
She sees when the sun awakens from her tent
Setting her paths ready for the journey ahead.

Her beauty is pure
With her charms she lures
She always has her way in any outpour.

She radiates with the rays of uniqueness
She is last born of God
Yet the backbone of every man.

The Survival of Adaku

She was born on the horizon of life
She faced war with no knife
Can she kill this lion like Samson with bare hands?

The world opened her eyes to see her down fall
Arms were closed for her not to stand tall
But she never stopped playing her ball.

Her dreams she never allowed to slumber
Her blessings she recalled in number
And her future will always escape hunger.

Like a towel she comforts herself by reaching the other
An Ada (first daughter) to mother
But a mother to another.

She is powerful
The force behind the door of motion
So elegant and industrious like an ant
The four elements of terra.

On her palm she bears the sun
Her heart is as open as the moon
Her eyes grant direction like the stars
She will positively affect the terrestrial like a virus.

Deception

Will I ever love again after this miss?
Will my heart still open to believe with all this diss
You made me feel comfort in your lies
I was captured by progression in deception.

Too lost in love to notice any misconception
My mind was twisted from the intake of observation
So fooling around as you toss with my emotion
I keep swimming deep into a love that was an illusion.

I will walk away quietly when I come to realization
Never to be bonded by frustration
But I will cast my gaze beyond your notion
Not because I am weak but I know there's no courage with fear.

I will walk Far away
From the reach of every molestation
To find the space where my heart will be given attention
I am endorsed with the right to always create an option.

The Shepherd's Rod

They may not be the head
But they are the stand on which the head was laid
To be brave and save
Giving her world a better place.

She holds up the house on her shoulder
Care and love are stored in her folder
With her our vision are made bolder
Beside all efforts she makes all come forth.

She is the sinew of recreation
Like the shepherd rod she grants direction
Like a tree she endures and ensures comfort
And like salt she gives taste and beauty to live's.

The Gold in Women

Judge not her weakness
From her insight lies uniqueness and meekness
Her bravery is a stone that has been uncovered
On her mind she carries the house.

She was crafted as an helper
For every pipe has its piper
Not to be scorned like a leper.

She is a mother and a wife
A child in the family (daughter)
A city you can pour your heart (friend)
For she is as smart as an eagle.

Behind every success
Behind the door of a shining star
Behind the shirt of a smiling belly
Behind the oasis of the healing air
There is a caring woman.

ABOUT THE AUTHOR

Matthew Edeh is a poet, a songwriter, and a playwright.
He is a student of public administration, still studying in his state university in Nigeria. He is known for passion for driving words and gives beauty to poetry. He mostly writes motivational, love, nature, and reality poems. When he's not writing he likes to sew and farm.

Visit Matthew on Facebook: @PenMysteries

Made in the USA
Middletown, DE
10 September 2021